MW01251260

Mi Amor
Spanish Recipes!

50 Perfect, Drop Dead Easy, Lip Smacking Delicious Spanish Cooking Recipes for You to Love Right Now

By Victoria Love

Your *Secret FREE Bonus!*

As a preferred client of Afflatus Publishing we strive to provide more value, all the time. As you are now a special part of our family we want to let you in on a little a little secret...

A special thanks goes out to you. So subscribe to our free e-book giveaway. Each week we will spotlight an amazing new title. Yours absolutely free.

Subscribe For Free Now
https://afflatus.leadpages.net/free-ebook/

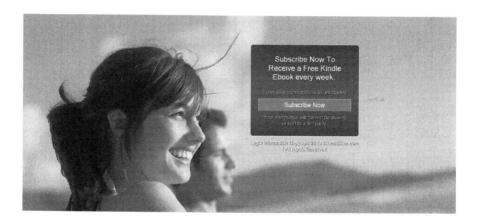

Table of Contents

Top 50 Spanish Main Dish, One Dish, Salad, Appetizer, Soup And Stew Meals

Spanish Soups and Stews

Spanish Salads

Spanish One Dishes

Spanish Appetizers

Spanish Main Dishes

Spanish Soups and Stews
Creamy Avocado Gazpacho

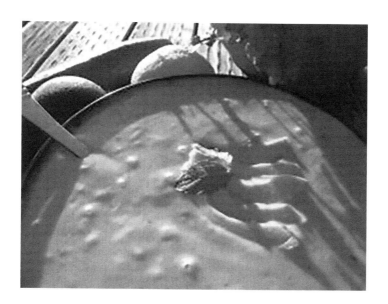

Ingredients

- 1 cup water
- 1 medium Avocado, flesh of, reserving 1 tables. For garnish
- 2 cups chopped cucumbers
- 1 1/2 cups chopped tomatoes
- 1/2-1 serrano chili, with seeds, sliced (optional)
- 1 large garlic clove, minced
- 1 sprig mint leaf
- 2 lemons, juice of or 2 limes, juice of

- 1/2 teaspoon salt
- 1 teaspoon maple syrup
- 2 small mint leaves
- Paprika (optional)

Directions

1. Blend everything together in processor till become smooth and creamy. Then after this, pour into soup bowls.

2. Take the preserved avocado and dice them and then drip them into the middle of bowl. Then take a mint leaf and add it and use the paprika as sprinkle all over diced avocado.

Castilian Garlic Soup

Ingredients

- 3 tablespoons extra virgin olive oil
- 6 garlic cloves, peeled and sliced
- 2 tablespoons white wine
- 1/2 tablespoon Spanish sweet paprika
- 3 ounces rustic white bread, crust removed and torn into small pieces
- 1 quart chicken stock
- 2 large eggs, beaten
- Salt
- 1 tablespoon flat leaf parsley, chopped

Directions

1. Fry the garlic in heated olive oil in saucepan over moderate temperature setting till become golden brown in color. Take the wine and add it and cook four and half minutes take the Spanish sweet paprika and add it and fry for sixty seconds.

2. Take the bread and add it and then after this, pour in chicken stock. Then blend well and heat to boiling and then lower the temperature and allow to simmer for eight minutes

3. Then blend in eggs and then after this fold them into soup and then allow to simmer for two minutes add the salt according to your own choice and use the parsley as sprinkle.

Pea Soup with Chorizo and Chipotle Peppers

Ingredients

- 1 tablespoon olive oil
- 1 onion, diced
- 1 celery, sliced
- 2 medium potatoes, diced
- 2 carrots, diced
- 2 garlic cloves, minced
- 1 teaspoon oregano
- 1/2-1 teaspoon pepper
- 1 bay leaf

- 1/2 lb chorizo sausage, sliced browned and grease discarded
- 1 (16 ounce) packages dried split peas
- Salt & pepper
- 1 -2 chipotle Chile in adobo, diced your choice to remove seeds
- Hot sauce (optional)

Directions

1. First of all, cook the carrot, potatoes, onions, and celery in heated oil for five minutes Then after this, take the salt, pepper, bay leaf, oregano, garlic and add them and cook for two minutes Then after this, take the peas, chipotles, sausage and add them and cover with water.

2. Heat to boiling and then lower the temperature and allow to simmer for approximately three to four hours or till become thick, mixing throughout the cooking.

3. Add the black pepper and hot pepper sauce and then use the croutons as garnish.

Pumpkin Chorizo Paella

Ingredients

- 1 lb chorizo sausage, removed from casings
- 1/2 cup onion, diced
- 2 garlic cloves, finely chopped
- 1 cup pumpkin, cooked
- 1/2 cup frozen peas
- 1/2 teaspoon cinnamon
- 1/2 teaspoon ground nutmeg
- 1/8 teaspoon ground cloves
- Fresh parsley
- Fresh snipped chives
- Roasted Tomatoes
- 2 medium Tomatoes, chopped
- 1 tablespoon honey
- Drizzle olive oil

- Salt and pepper
- Saffron Rice
- 4 cups chicken broth
- 1 pinch saffron thread
- 1 cup Arborio rice

Directions

1. 1st For Roasted Tomatoes: take the olive oil, salt, pepper, honey, and chopped tomatoes and toss them together and put on baking sheet that has been greased and roast in oven at three hundred twenty five (325) degrees Fahrenheit for 1/3 hour.

2. 2nd For Saffron Rice: heat the chicken broth to boiling. Take the Arborio rice, saffron and add them and heat back to boiling. Then lower to simmer and allow to simmer, covered for 1/3 hour don't drain the rice prior to adding to paella mixture.

3. 3rd For Paella: take the garlic, onion, sausage and cook them in sauté pan over moderately high temperature and then break the sausage into chunks and then when brown, then blend in saffron rice, then blend in roasted tomatoes then blend in pumpkin. Then blend in peas and then blend in spices. Allow to simmer for five to ten minutes use the chives and parsley as garnishes

Slow Cooker Easy Spicy Sausage Soup

Ingredients

- 1 lb extra lean ground beef
- 1 lb spicy bulk sausage (casings removed)
- 1/2 large onion, chopped
- 2 cups carrots, chopped
- 2 cups celery, chopped
- 1 bell pepper, chopped (red or green)
- Salt and pepper
- 1 teaspoon dried oregano
- 2 -3 garlic cloves, minced
- 14 1/2 ounces stewed tomatoes and green chilies
- 14 1/2 ounces green beans
- 1/4 teaspoon chili powder
- 1 cup instant rice, uncooked

Directions

1. Take the onions, sausage, and beef and mix them together and then roll into ball shapes. Then use the pam for coating the crock pot and put the meatballs in it.

2. Blend the rest of items besides rice and then right after this, pour over meatballs. Then cook, covered, over low temperature setting for six to eight hours then blend in rice in the final twenty minutes of cooking.

Spanish Army Soup

Ingredients

- 2 tablespoons olive oil
- 1 clove garlic, crushed
- 1/2 onion, finely diced
- 1/2 green capsicum, finely diced
- 2 Tomatoes, chopped
- 500 g rump steak, cubed
- 5 large potatoes, cubed into medium sized chunks
- 3 carrots, sliced
- 1/2 Japanese pumpkin, chopped into large chunks
- 2 tablespoons paprika

- Salt and pepper
- 2 teaspoons beef stock powder
- 7 cups water
- 1/2 teaspoon powdered imitation saffron
- 1 bay leaf
- 1/4 cup dry sherry

Directions

1. Fry the tomato, capsicum, garlic, and onion in heated oil in pot. Take the beef and add it and cook till become brown in color. Take sherry and add it and allow to reduce little bit and then after this, you can add some water for covering up beef.

2. Allow to simmer for 1/3 hour. Take the remaining items and add them along with water and heat to boiling. Then reduce the temperature and allow to simmer for next sixty minutes or till potatoes become tender and soup become thick.

Crock Pot -Chicken Tortilla Soup

Ingredients

- 1 lb shredded cooked chicken
- 1 (15 ounce) cans whole canned tomatoes, mashed
- 1 (10 ounce) cans enchilada sauce
- 1 medium onion, chopped
- 1 (4 ounce) cans chopped green chili peppers
- 2 garlic cloves, minced
- 1 cup water
- 1 (14 1/2 ounce) cans chicken broth
- 1 teaspoon cumin
- 1 teaspoon chili powder

- 1 teaspoon salt
- 1/4 teaspoon black pepper
- 1 bay leaf
- 1 (10 ounce) packages frozen corn
- 1 tablespoon chopped fresh cilantro

Directions

1. Take the chicken, garlic, green chilies, onion, enchilada sauce, tomatoes and put them into slow cooker. Then after this, take chicken broth, water and pour them in.

2. Add the bay leaf, salt, pepper, chili powder and cuminutes, then blend in cilantro and blend in corn.

3. Then cook, covered, on high temperature for three to four minutes use the tortilla chips as garnish.

Canary Island Cilantro Soup

Ingredients

- 1 medium onion, finely minced
- 1 ripe Tomato, peeled and seeded, finely chopped
- 2 cloves garlic, mashed
- 3 medium potatoes, peeled and diced roughly
- 1/4 cup rice
- 1 bunch fresh cilantro, divided
- 1 green pepper, cut in half
- 2 bouillon cubes
- 1 pinch sea salt
- 1/2 teaspoon paprika
- 2 tablespoons olive oil
- 1 1/2 quarts water, enough to cover vegetables

Directions

1. Fry the paprika, potatoes, tomato, garlic and onion in two tbsp heated olive oil in soup pot over high temperature setting till onions become translucent.

2. Take the bouillon, half of green pepper, two third of bunch of cilantro, tied with string and add them and add salt according to your own choice. Take water and add enough of it to cover the veggies and heat to boiling and then lower the temperature and allow to simmer for approximately ½ hour.

3. Then add the rice once half way through the cooking time. Don't forget to adjust seasoning and remove the bunch of cilantro and green pepper. Take the rest of green pepper and chop them along with cilantro.

Easy Black Bean Soup

Ingredients

- 3 tablespoons olive oil
- 1 medium onion, chopped
- 1 tablespoon ground cumin
- 2 -3 cloves garlic
- 2 (14 1/2 ounce) cans black beans
- 2 cups chicken broth or 2 cups vegetable broth
- Salt and pepper
- 1 small red onion, chopped fine
- 1/4 cup cilantro, coarsely chopped or finely chopped

Directions

1. Take the onion and fry it in olive oil till become translucent. Take cumin and add it. Then cook for four and half minutes take garlic and add it and cook for next half minute take two cups of veggie broth, one can of black beans and add them.

2. Then heat to simmer, mixing from time to time. Then turn down the temperature. Then mix the items in pot. Take the 2nd beans can and add it to the pot.

3. Take the mixed items and add them and heat to simmer. You can serve this delicious recipe with bowls of red onion and cilantro.

Spanish Kale Soup

Ingredients

- 1 bunch kale
- 1/2 head green cabbage
- 6 -8 cups chicken stock or 6 -8 cups canned reduced-sodium chicken broth
- 1 lb. linguae sausage, sliced 1/4 inch thick
- 1 lb red potatoes, diced
- 2 (15 1/4 ounce) cans dark red kidney beans
- 1 (14 1/2 ounce) cans diced tomatoes
- 1 medium onion, chopped
- 3 garlic cloves, minced
- 2 teaspoons crushed red pepper flakes
- 3 bay leaves

- 1/8 teaspoon Hungarian paprika
- 1 -2 tablespoon olive oil
- Coarse salt
- Fresh ground black pepper

Directions

1. First of all, wash the kale and then strip from firm stem and then chop and put aside. Then after this, take cabbage and shred it in blender and then drain and rinse the beans.

2. Cook the minced garlic, chopped onion, sausage in heated olive oil in stock pot till become transparent, mixing from time to time.

3. Take rest of items and add them and heat to boiling and then lower the temperature and allow to simmer for ¾ to 1 hour. Then after this, season with salt as well as pepper according to your own choice. Then discard the bay leaf.

Spanish Salads

Garlic Thyme Potato Tapas

Ingredients

- 3 lbs potatoes
- 1 tablespoon Dijon mustard
- 1/3 cup mayonnaise
- 2 garlic cloves, finely chopped
- 1 tablespoon fresh thyme, finely chopped
- 1 teaspoon black pepper
- 1/4 cup green onion, finely chopped

Directions

1. Take the potatoes and peel them and then chop them and then boil them till ready and done. Then drain them and then cool them.

2. Then after this, take mayonnaise, garlic, thyme, pepper, mustard and blend them together in bowl.

3. Then blend in potatoes. Then blend in onions. Then allow to chill in refrigerator for a minimum of sixty minutes

Mixed Pepper Salad

Ingredients

- 2 red bell peppers, halved and seeded
- 2 yellow bell peppers, halved and seeded
- 2 tablespoons olive oil, DIVIDED
- 1 onion, thinly sliced
- 2 garlic cloves, crushed
- 1/8 teaspoon pepper
- 1 dash salt
- Lemon juice, generous squeeze
- Fresh parsley, chopped for garnish

Directions

1. Take the pepper halves and broil them for five minutes or till skin become black and blister and then after this, you can pop them into plastic bag and then seal and let it sit for five minutes then sauté the onion in one tbsp of olive oil in skillet for six minutes or till become tender.

2. Take away from heat and preserve. Then remove the peppers from bag and peel their skins and then remove the pepper skins and chop each one of the pepper half into fine strips. Then take cooked onions, peppers, any oil from pan, and put them in a bowl.

3. Take the salt, pepper, crushed garlic, one tbsp of olive oil, squeeze of lemon juice and add them season according to your own choice. Then blend well and allow to marinate, covered, for three hours, mixing two times. Then use the chopped parsley as garnish.

Spanish Asparagus Salad with Orange and Manchego Cheese

Ingredients

- 1 cup fresh asparagus spear
- 2 medium oranges
- 1/2 cup red onion, sliced and cut into crescents
- 2 Tomatoes, ripe but firm, cut into eighths
- 3 cups romaine leaves, chopped into narrow strips
- 2 ounces manchego cheese, for garnish (optional)
- Salad Dressing
- 2 tablespoons extra virgin olive oil
- 1 tablespoon sherry wine vinegar
- 1/2 orange, zest of, finely minced
- 1 tablespoon reserved orange juice
- Salt
- Fresh ground black pepper

Directions

1. First of all, blanch asparagus spears in pot of salted and boiling water till become green in color. Then drain and rinse. Then take oranges and peel them and chop them into pieces.

2. Take the one tbsp of orange juice, orange zest, olive oil, vinegar, salt, pepper and mix them together in a bowl and put aside.

3. Take the lettuce, tomatoes, cooked asparagus, red onion, orange pieces and mix them together. Take the dressing and pour this over the salad and toss well. Then you can also add the shavings of manchego to each of the serving.

Valencia Corn Salad

Ingredients

- Salad
- 3 cups corn
- 1 (2 ounce) jars pimientos, drained or 2 ounces roasted red peppers
- 1/2 cup sliced black olives, drained
- 1/4 cup red onion, diced small
- 2 tablespoons fresh curly-leaf parsley, minced
- Vinaigrette
- 1/2 cup freshly squeezed orange juice
- 3 tablespoons apple cider vinegar
- 2 tablespoons extra virgin olive oil
- 1 small pinch Spanish smoked paprika
- Salt, to taste
- Fresh ground black pepper, to taste

Directions

1. First of all, whisk vinaigrette items. Take it and pour this over the corn mixture and toss well.

2. Then allow to chill, covered, till serving time.

Baby Spinach and Lentil Salad

Ingredients

- 1 cup dried brown lentils
- 3 cups vegetable stock
- 2 bay leaves
- 1 (3 inch) cinnamon sticks
- 2 garlic cloves, minced
- 1/2 medium white onion, chopped
- 1/4 cup Kalamata olive, chopped
- 1/2 medium green bell pepper, diced
- 2 medium roma tomatoes, diced
- 1/2 medium carrot, scrubbed and shredded
- 2 tablespoons parsley, chopped

- 1 lemon, juice of
- 2 tablespoons extra virgin olive oil
- 2 teaspoons fresh thyme leaves or 1/2 teaspoon dried thyme leaves
- 1/2 teaspoon fennel seed
- 1/2 teaspoon oregano
- 1/2 teaspoon crushed red pepper flakes
- 1/2 cup feta cheese, crumbled
- Salt
- Pepper
- 10 ounces Baby Spinach

Directions

1. First of all, take the lentils, sort them and wash them in put them in pan and then add the stock, cinnamon stick and bay leaf. Then heat to boiling and lower the temperature and allow to simmer for 1/3 hour or till become soft, then drain well and remove the cinnamon stick as well as bay leaf.

2. Then fry the garlic and onions in two tbsp of lentil cooking liquid in sauté pan till become tender and slightly brown in color. Take the lentils and put them in bowl. And then after this, you can add the olives through parsley. Then blend in cooked garlic. Then blend in cooked onion then blend in lentil mixture.

3. Then use the lemon juice and olive oil for drizzling. Blend in feta cheese and then blend in salt as well as pepper. Then allow to chill for a couple of minutes then distribute the salad greens into dishes and use the lentil salad mixture for topping.

Spanish Chickpea Salad

Ingredients

- 1/2 kg chickpeas
- 1 large Tomato
- 4 red peppers
- 50 g cured ham, diced
- Hard-boiled egg, chopped
- 1 bunch spring onion, sliced
- 1 small garlic clove
- Extra virgin olive oil
- White wine vinegar
- Salt and pepper
- Fresh parsley

Directions

1. First of all, take the chickpeas and drain them and then rinse them.

2. Then after this, prepare the tomato by blanching the tomato and then get rid of the skin and pips and then chop it into cubes and then put them in bowl.

3. Take the red peppers, eggs, garlic, onion, chopped cured ham and add them all to the bowl. Then use the white wine vinegar and olive oil for dressing and add the salt and pepper. Take the chickpeas and add them to the mixture of salad.

Spanish Citrus Salad

Ingredients

- 3 large oranges, peeled and sectioned
- 15 ounces canned red kidney beans, drained
- 1/2 cup celery, chopped
- 1 small onion, sliced and separated into rings
- 1 tablespoon parsley, snipped
- 1 tablespoon pimiento, chopped
- 1/3 cup unsweetened grapefruit juice
- 1/4 cup salad oil
- 1 tablespoon vinegar
- 1/2 teaspoon salt
- 1/4 teaspoon dried oregano, crushed
- 1/8 teaspoon dried thyme, crushed
- 5 -6 romaine leaves, for garnish

Directions

1. First of all, chop the orange and chop its sections into half crosswise. Then after this, take the pimiento, parsley, onion, celery, kidney beans, and oranges and blend them together in a bowl.

2. Then mix the rest of items and then pour this over the mixture in the bowl

3. Then allow to chill in refrigerator for a couple of hours, mixing couple of times.

Zucchini Salad

Ingredients

- 4 tablespoons olive oil
- 1 clove garlic, halved
- 500 g small zucchini, sliced 1 cm thick
- 1/2 cup pine nuts, toasted
- 1/2 cup raisins
- 3 tablespoons finely chopped mint
- 2 tablespoons lemon juice, to taste
- Salt and pepper

Directions

1. Fry the halved garlic clove in heated oil till become brown in color and then take out then after this, take zucchini and add it to pan and fry till soft and brown in color.

2. Then flip the zucchini and oil in the bowl and then add the rest of items then after this, let it cool and then allow to cool, covered for a minimum of 180 minutes

3. Take out of fridge approximately ¼ hour.

Andalusian Rice Salad

Ingredients

- 1 cup rice
- 1 teaspoon salt
- 8 tablespoons olive oil
- 3 tablespoons wine vinegar
- 1 large garlic clove, minced
- 1 small onion, minced
- Salt and pepper, to taste
- 1 (4 ounce) jars piquillo peppers, whole, drained and sliced in strips
- 4 sprigs parsley, finely chopped
- Green olives, for garnish
- Pitted black olives, for garnish

Directions

1. First of all, heat two cup of water to boiling. Take a pinch of salt, rice and add them, then cook, covered, for HALF hour or till rice become soft and then allow to cool the rice.

2. Prepare vinaigrette sauce, by mixing the onion, garlic, vinegar and olive oil. Then add the salt and pepper according to your own choice.

3. Take the rice and mix it with olives, parsley, peppers and vinaigrette sauce in a bowl.

Ensalada Mixta

Ingredients

- 1 head romaine lettuce
- 2 medium Tomatoes
- 1 small red onion
- 1/2 cucumber
- 1 Avocado
- 1 (7 ounce) cans corn, drained
- 1 can tuna, drained
- 1/4 cup olive
- Extra virgin olive oil
- Red wine vinegar
- Salt and pepper

Directions

1. First of all, chop the lettuce and organize over a dish. Then chop the tomatoes in wedges along with sliced avocado, sliced cucumber and onion julienne and organize over the lettuce.

2. Then after this, break the tuna and put in the middle of salad. Then drain the corn and then after this, organize around the tuna. Then use the olives as garnish.

Spanish One Dishes
Zarangollo Murciano

Ingredients

- 6 tablespoons olive oil
- 2 garlic cloves, minced
- 3 yellow onions, finely chopped
- 2 lbs zucchini, diced small
- Salt, pepper
- 2 teaspoons oregano
- 6 eggs (optional)

Directions

1. First of all, sauté the onions and garlic in half of the oil in skillet for approximately ¼ hour or till become tender.

2. Then fry the zucchini in the rest of oil in another skillet for approximately ¼ hour or till become tender. Then drain and add this to onion in skillet.

3. Then add the oregano, pepper and salt and keep on cooking for approximately five minutes

Seafood Paella

Ingredients

- 3 pinches saffron threads
- 3 tablespoons olive oil
- 1 large onion, sliced into rings
- 10 ounces rice
- 3 Tomatoes, cubed
- 2 garlic cloves, chopped
- 16 1/2 ounces chicken broth
- 16 mussels, scrubbed, debearded
- 16 prawns
- 4 crab claws
- 12 small littleneck clams, scrubbed
- 6 ounces white fish fillets, cubed
- 4 ounces peas
- 1 red pepper, sliced

Directions

1. First of all, take the saffron and soak into two tablespoons of hot water. Then after this, fry the onions in Dutch oven for four minutes Take the saffron, rice and add them and fry for two minutes, mixing continuously.

2. Take the chicken broth, garlic, tomatoes and add them and heat to boiling then reduce the temperature and you can then add half of the all seafood along with red pepper and peas.

3. Then after this, add the salt and pepper and blend them. Take the remaining seafood and add them over the top and then use the parchment paper for covering and cover it and allow to simmer for ½ hour. Then let it rest for five minutes, uncovered.

Spanish Style Tomato with Ham

Ingredients

- 1 crusty long roll
- 2 Tomatoes, roma size
- 2 drizzles of extra-virgin olive oil
- 2 thin slices ham
- 2 slices manchego cheese

Directions

1. Take the roll and chop it in half and then toast it to get little bit brown in color all over then after this, use the olive oil to drizzle over the bread.

2. Then after this, squeeze the tomato all over the bread. Do the same on the other side of bread.

3. Use the fine cheese slice as topping for each half. Then after this, use the finely sliced dry cured ham for topping each of the roll.

White Melon Sangria

Ingredients

- 1 1/2 cups melon, pieces
- 1/3 cup sugar
- 1 (750 ml) bottles crisp white wine, such as Sauvignon Blanc or 1 (750 ml) bottles pinot grigio wine
- 1/4 cup brandy
- 2 tablespoons triple sec or 2 tablespoons other orange-flavored liqueur
- 3/4 cup sparkling water or 3/4 cup club soda
- Ice cube
- Limes or star fruit, slices (to garnish)
- 1 small mint sprig (to garnish)

Directions

1. Take the sugar, melon and blend them together in a pitcher and then allow to rest for approximately ¼ to ½ hour for drawing out juices.

2. Take the triple sec, sparkling water, brandy, wine and blend them together into pitcher. Then take ice cubes and add them to six glasses.

3. Then after this, use sangria for filling the glasses and then use some of the fruit for spooning over every glass. Then use the lime slice as garnish for each along with mint sprig.

Blender Gazpacho

Ingredients

- 2 lbs ripe Tomatoes, peeled, seeded, and coarsely chopped or 1 (28 ounce) cans best-quality plum tomatoes, chopped
- 1 medium sweet onion, coarsely chopped
- 1 large cucumber, peeled and coarsely chopped
- 1/2 green bell pepper, coarsely chopped
- 1/2 red bell pepper, coarsely chopped
- 2 scallions, coarsely chopped
- 3 garlic cloves
- 1/3 cup extra virgin olive oil
- 3 tablespoons sherry wine vinegar or 3 tablespoons balsamic vinegar
- 1 -2 teaspoon hot pepper sauce
- 1 teaspoon ground cumin
- 1/2-1 cup chilled tomato juice

- Salt & freshly ground black pepper, to taste
- Garnishes
- Croutons or chopped fresh herbs or sliced scallions or diced Avocado

Directions

1. Take the garlic, scallions, tomatoes, onion, bell peppers, cucumber and blend them together in a bowl then after this, whirl the mixture in processor till chopped finely. Then bring the mixture back to bowl.

2. Then blend in olive oil. Then blend in vinegar. Then blend in hot pepper sauce. Then blend in cuminutes Take cold tomato juice and add enough of it for making the gazpacho soupy. Then add the salt as well as pepper.

3. Then keep the bowl, covered, in refrigerator. Then after this, pour into bowls. Use the croutons, scallions and herbs as garnishes.

Spanish Doughnuts

Ingredients

- 4 tablespoons butter, cut in pieces
- 1/2 cup water
- 1/8 teaspoon salt
- 1 1/4 cups all-purpose flour
- 3 eggs
- 1/4 teaspoon vanilla
- Oil, for frying
- 1/2 teaspoon cinnamon
- 1/2 cup sugar

Directions

1. Blend the water and butter in saucepan and heat to boiling. Then after this, you can add the salt and take away from heat. Then beat in the flour. Then bring back to heat and beat well and then take away from heat. And allow to cool.

2. Then after this, you can beat in the egg. Then blend in vanilla till mixture become satiny. Then after this, take the mixture and press it through cookie press. Then chop it into strips.

3. Then sauté for two minutes at three hundred fifty (35o) degrees Fahrenheit per side. Then drain well and then after this, roll in cinnamon and sugar mixture.

Spanish Magdelenas-Madeleines

Ingredients

- 17 teaspoons cornstarch
- 34 teaspoons all-purpose flour
- 35 teaspoons white sugar
- 6 tablespoons milk
- 125 ml vegetable oil
- 2 eggs
- 1 tablespoon baking powder
- 1 tablespoon kirsch
- 1 lemon, zest of

Directions

1. Take the eggs, sugar and beat them together till fluffy. Then after this, add the rest of items.

2. Then after this, fill the muffin paper tins and then bake for 1/3 hour at three hundred fifty (35o) degrees Fahrenheit or till become golden in color.

3. Then allow to cool and then keep in airtight container.

Spanish Melonball

Ingredients

- 1 ounce coconut rum
- 1 ounce Midori melon liqueur
- 1 ounce pineapple juice
- 3 ounces orange juice
- Ice

Directions

1. Take the pineapple juice, Malibu, Midori and shake them well and then strain into a glass. Take the orange juice and add it.

Spanish Olive & Cream Cheese Canapés

Ingredients

- 10 slices bread
- 1 1/2 tablespoons unsalted butter, melted
- 1 ounce Parmigiano-Reggiano cheese
- 6 ounces cream cheese, softened
- 1/3 cup Spanish olives
- 1/4 cup scallion, finely chopped
- 1/4 cup red bell pepper, finely chopped
- 1/4 teaspoon sweet paprika
- 2 teaspoons medium-dry sherry

Directions

1. First of all, chop FORTY round shapes from the slices of bread and then after this, brush one side of each of the round with the butter and then bake on baking sheet till become pale golden in color. Then take out of oven.

2. Then right after this, take the Parmigiano-Reggiano and finely grate it. Take the sherry, paprika, cream cheese, olives, scallions, bell pepper and mash them together.

3. Then use one teaspoon of cheese mixture for topping each of the toast. And use the grated Parmigiano-Reggiano as sprinkle. Then after this, broil canapés till Parmigiano-Reggiano starts to become golden in color.

Grilled Halibut with Peppers and Artichokes

Ingredients

- 1 yellow bell pepper, sliced
- 4 roma tomatoes, chopped
- 1 large onion, chopped
- 1 cup artichoke heart, canned, drain and quarter
- 8 garlic cloves, minced
- 1 tablespoon smoked paprika
- Kosher salt
- 1/2 cup dry white wine
- 1 lemon, thinly sliced
- 4 halibut fillets (5-6oz each)
- Chopped fresh parsley

Directions

1. Take the salt, bell pepper, paprika, tomatoes, garlic, onion, and artichoke hearts and blend them together in a bowl. Then blend in wine. Then after this, chop the foil into four pieces and then after this, fold each sheet in half for making a double layer.

2. Then after this, distribute the vegetables into four sections. Then put on section in the middle of every foil piece. Take the fish fillet and put this on veggies in each of the packet. Then use the lemon slices for topping.

3. Then keep on folding till packet is sealed. Then roll them together towards the middle for sealing. Then grill these packets, covered, for ten minutes take away from heat and then unfold.

Spanish Appetizers

Black Bean Gazpacho

Ingredients

- 7 (16 ounce) cans black beans, drained
- 2 (4 ounce) jars capers, drained
- 1 large raw yellow onion, grated
- 1 small raw yellow onion, grated
- 3 (4 ounce) jars sliced pimientos, drained, rinsed
- 3 teaspoons cumin
- 4 tablespoons cilantro
- 3 limes, juice of
- 3 (8 ounce) cans green chilies, chopped variety
- 13 cups regular flavor V8 vegetable juice
- 6 tablespoons extra virgin olive oil

- 6 tablespoons Worcestershire sauce
- 1 1/2 cups garlic
- 3 tablespoons balsamic vinegar
- 2 (12 ounce) jars medium heat salsa
- 1 (6 ounce) jars bottle hot salsa
- 3 large chopped cucumbers

Directions

1. Take the V8 juice, beans, garlic, Worcestershire, onion, cucumber, lime juice, oil etc and blend them together and then put into pots for mixing. Then allow to chill for a couple of minutes

2. You can serve this delicious recipe with corn tortillas.

Shrimp in Green Mayonnaise

Ingredients

- 1/4 cup mayonnaise
- 1/4 cup fresh parsley, minced
- 2 teaspoons capers, finely chopped
- 1/4 teaspoon dried oregano
- 1 lb. medium shrimp (31-40 shrimp, cooked, peeled, deveined, and thawed if frozen)

Directions

1. Take the oregano, capers, parsley, and mayonnaise and blend them together in a bowl.
2. Take the shrimp and add it to bowl and blend till thoroughly blended.
3. Then keep in refrigerator.

Lemon Olive Tapas

Ingredients

- 1 pint good green olives (or both mixed) or 1 pint black olives (or both mixed)
- 1/4 teaspoon kosher salt
- 1/2 teaspoon black peppercorns
- 3 bay leaves
- 3 sprigs fresh rosemary or 3 sprigs fresh thyme
- 1/2 teaspoon fennel seed, lightly crushed
- 4 -5 garlic cloves, cut in half lengthwise
- 1 pinch dried red pepper flakes (optional)
- 2 medium lemons
- 3 tablespoons extra virgin olive oil

Directions

1. Take the garlic, red pepper flakes, olives, salt, herb sprigs, fennel seeds, peppercorns, bay leaves and mix them together in a bowl.

2. Then after this, zest your lemons and then add the oil & zest to olives and blend properly well.

3. Then after this, pour and scrape into a jar that is covered and keep in refrigerator for TWELVE hours to twenty four hours.

Spicy Pork Skewers (Pinchos Morunos)

Ingredients

- 1 pork tenderloin (about 1 pound)
- 2 tablespoons sweet paprika
- 1 teaspoon ground cumin
- 1 teaspoon cayenne, to taste
- Salt and pepper, to taste
- 6 -8 tablespoons olive oil

Directions

1. First of all, chop the pork tenderloin into cubes. Take the olive oil, pepper, salt, cayenne, paprika, cumin and blend them together in a bowl and then allow the marinate the pork for a minimum of four minutes

2. Then after this, take the pork cubes and thread them onto wooden skewers and bake for approximately ¼ hour at three hundred fifty (350) degrees Fahrenheit.

3. When this recipe is cooking, you should turn one time and use the marinade for basting till become brown in color.

Warm Manchego Cheese Popovers

Ingredients

- 2 eggs, beaten
- 1 cup milk
- 2 tablespoons butter, melted (no substitutes)
- 1 cup all-purpose flour
- 1/2 teaspoon salt
- 1 dash pepper
- 2 ounces manchego cheese, finely shredded (1/2 cup)
- 2 tablespoons cilantro, snipped
- 1 tablespoon chopped pimento-stuffed green olives
- Nonstick cooking spray

Directions

1. Use the cooking spray for coating the twenty four muffins cups and put them aside. Take the salt, pepper, eggs, milk, butter and mix them together. Take the olives, cilantro, and cheese and add them.

2. Then after this, fill the muffin cups with this mixture and bake for approximately ¼ hour at four hundred twenty five (425) degrees Fahrenheit or till become golden brown in color.

Champinones Al Ajillo

Ingredients

- 5 tablespoons olive oil
- 2 tablespoons minced garlic
- 1 lb assorted fresh mushrooms, cleaned and halved
- 1/4 cup dry white wine
- 1/4 cup fresh parsley
- Salt and pepper

Directions

1. Fry the garlic in heated oil in skillet over moderate temperature setting for 120 seconds. Then after this, high temperature and add your mushrooms and fry them till become soft, mixing from time to time.

2. Take the wine, and add it and keep on cooking till liquid is absorbed. Take the parsley and add it along with pepper, and salt and mix well.

Cod & Potato Tapas

Ingredients

- 1 1/4 lbs salt cod fish
- 5 cups unsalted potatoes (riced or finely mashed)
- 1/2 cup finely chopped onion
- 1/3 cup finely chopped fresh parsley
- 4 teaspoons lemon juice
- 1/4 teaspoon nutmeg
- 1/4 teaspoon pepper
- 3 eggs, beaten
- Oil (for deep frying)

Directions

1. First of all, put the rinsed, soaked and drained cod in saucepan. Then add the water in the saucepan to cover the cod and heat to boiling. Then allow to simmer till fish flakes easily, approximately ¼ hour. Then right after this, drain well and allow to cool and then remove the bones and skin.

2. Then after this, shred it finely in blender. Take the nutmeg, cod, potatoes, onion, parsley, lemon juice, pepper and mix them and adjust seasoning according to your own choice. Then blend in eggs.

3. Then after this, scoop up heaping spoonful of cod mixture. Then scoop the 2nd spoonful over the 1st one and make rounded oval like shape that will let the additional to fall back in the bowl and then put on tray. Do the same with remaining mixture. Then after this, sauté the ovals in heated oil till become crunchy and golden in color and then drain well.

Tuna & Olive Croquettes

Ingredients

- 2 tablespoons butter
- 1 medium onion, minced
- 1/4 cup all-purpose flour
- 1 (7 ounce) cans tuna in water
- Milk
- Salt & freshly ground black pepper
- 1/2 cup pimento stuffed olive
- 1/4 cup minced parsley
- 2 tablespoons capers, minced (optional)
- Flour, for coating

- 2 eggs, beaten
- Breadcrumbs, for coating
- Vegetable oil (for frying)

Directions

1. Fry the onion in melted butter in saucepan over moderate temperature setting till become tender. Then blend in flour and cook for sixty seconds.

2. Then right after this, drain tuna and measure the liquid. Take milk and add enough of it to equal one FORTH cup of liquid. Then after this, whisk into the mixture of flour and cook till become thick. Add the salt and pepper and blend in olives then blend in tuna and then keep the mixture in refrigerator till become cold.

3. Then make patty from the one fourth cup of mixture and then right this coat with the flour and then coat with the egg and then coat with the bread crumbs.

4. Then sauté in heated oil in sauté pan, turning one or two times or till become golden in color on the outer side and crunchy as well.

Mussels with Chorizo, Tomato and Wine

Ingredients

- 8 ounces chorizo sausage, casings removed & chopped
- 3 tablespoons unsalted butter
- 1 yellow onion, finely chopped
- 1 shallot, finely chopped
- 1/2 teaspoon fennel seed
- 1/2 teaspoon fresh ground black pepper
- 3 garlic cloves, minced
- 7 roma tomatoes, peeled, seeded and chopped
- 3/4 cup white wine
- 1/2 cup heavy cream

- 2 tablespoons finely chopped fresh parsley leaves
- 4 lbs fresh mussels, scrubbed & debearded
- French bread

Directions

1. First of all, fry the chorizo in skillet over moderately high temperature setting till become brown in color, approximately four minutes then drain well and then after this, drain off all however one tbsp of fat from pan. Then after this, cook the fennel seeds, pepper, shallot and onions in melted butter, mixing, till vegetables become soft.

2. Take the garlic, tomatoes and add them and cook, mixing for 120 seconds. Then take the mussels and add them to pan. Take the wine, one fourth cup of cream, parsley and add them and heat to boiling. Blend the mussels and cook, covered, till the shells are open, for approximately eight minutes

3. Then take the mussels out of pan to serving bowls and then after this, remove those shells which are not open. Then after this, heat the pan with juice to boiling and then let it boil for three minutes take the cream, sausage and add them and heat to boiling for sixty seconds. Then after this, take the juice and pour this over the mussels.

Paprika Potatoes

Ingredients

- 1 kg small potato
- 2 tablespoons olive oil
- Sea salt
- SAUCE
- 4 tablespoons olive oil
- 1 tablespoon tomato puree
- 1 tablespoon red wine vinegar
- 2 tablespoons water
- 1 teaspoon chili sauce
- 2 teaspoons paprika
- Salt and pepper

Directions

1. Slice the potatoes and put them in one layer on baking sheet. Then after this, use the olive oil for brushing. Use the sea salt as sprinkle and then after this, roast at four hundred fifty (45o) degrees Fahrenheit for approximately 1/3 hour then flip and bake for next ten minutes or till golden in color and crunchy.

2. Then after this, take the sauce items and mix them together in skillet, mixing well.

3. Take the cooked potatoes and add them and heat through and add the salt and pepper.

Spanish Main Dishes

Cerdo De Barcelona

Ingredients

- 2 tablespoons olive oil, divided
- 10 ounces vermicelli or 10 ounces spaghetti, broken into 2 inch pieces
- 1 1/2 lbs boneless pork chops, cut into bite size pieces
- 2 1/2 cups onions, chopped
- 1 tablespoon garlic, minced
- 8 ounces fresh chorizo sausage, no casing
- 2 (14 1/2 ounce) cans fire roasted diced tomatoes, undrained (Hunts)
- 1 2/3 cups reduced-sodium chicken broth
- 1 1/2 teaspoons paprika
- 1/4 teaspoon salt
- 1/4 teaspoon ground red pepper

Directions

1. First of all, sauté and mix the broken vermicelli in one tbsp of oil in sauté pan over moderately high temperature till become light brown in color. Take out from sauté and put aside.

2. Then after this, sauté the pork in rest of one tbsp of oil in sauté pan till each side become light brown in color. Then take out the pork and vermicelli from sauté pan.

3. Take the garlic, onions and add them to sauté pan and cook till onions become tender, mixing from time to time. Take the chorizo and add them and cook till crumbly, mixing from time to time. Then blend in pepper as well as salt, then blend in undrained tomatoes. Then blend in broth. Then blend in paprika and heat to boiling. Then bring the vermi- celli and pork back to sauté pan and cook till vermicelli is ready and done, mixing from time to time.

Spanish Delicious Pisto

Ingredients

- 1 small onion, chopped
- 1 1/2 garlic cloves, minced
- 2 tablespoons olive oil
- 2 medium Tomatoes, peeled and chopped
- 1 medium zucchini, sliced
- 1 small eggplant, unpeeled and cubed
- 1 small green pepper, cut into strips
- 1 small sweet red pepper, cut into strips
- 1/2 cup ham, fully cooked and diced
- 1/4 cup dry sherry
- 1/2 teaspoon dried basil, crushed
- 1/4 teaspoon salt
- 1/4 teaspoon pepper

Directions

1. Fry the garlic and onion in sauté pan in heated oil till become soft. Then after this, blend in tomatoes. Then blend in zucchini slices and then blend in eggplant cubes and then blend in green pepper strips and then blend in red pepper strips. Then blend in ham. Then blend sherry.

2. Then blend in salt and then blend in pepper and then blend in basil. Then cook, covered, for approximately. five minutes or till zucchini as well as eggplant become soft.

3. Then use the egg and mix it into mixture.

Onion-Smothered Steak

Ingredients

- 2 tablespoons red wine vinegar
- 2 teaspoons garlic, minced
- 1 1/2 teaspoons sweet paprika
- 1/2 teaspoon salt, plus salt to taste
- 1/2 teaspoon ground pepper, freshly ground
- 32 ounces rib eye steaks (4 each 8 oz. steaks)
- 1/4 cup olive oil
- 2 cups yellow onions, chopped
- 1/2 cup canned plum tomatoes, diced
- 1 bay leaf
- 1/4 cup tawny port
- 3 tablespoons Italian parsley, chopped

Directions

1. Take the half teaspoon of salt, half teaspoon of pepper, one tablespoon of vinegar, one tablespoon of garlic, paprika and blend them together in a bowl to make a paste. Then right after this, use this paste for rubbing on both of the sides of steaks and put them aside for marinating for sixty minutes

2. Then fry the onion in heated olive oil in skillet over moderate temperature setting, mixing from time to time or till become golden in color, approximately. twenty five minutes take the rest of teaspoon of garlic, tomato, rest of vinegar, bay leaf, pork and add them and allow to simmer for ten minutes over moderate temperature.

3. Then add the salt and pepper according to your own choice and then blend in parsley. Take away from heat. Then heat two sauté pans over high temperature and use salt as sprinkle over both of them and then cook the steaks over high temperature, turning one time, five minutes per side for rare or till preferred doneness is achieved. Take the tomato onion sauce and add it and heated through, turning the steaks in sauce.

Spanish Spinach Omelette

Ingredients

- 14 ounces spinach leaves
- 3 tablespoons olive oil
- 1 large onion, finely sliced
- 2 large potatoes, peeled and finely sliced
- 10 eggs

Directions

4. Take the spinach and tip it into colander and heat a kettle of water to boiling. Then after this, take the water and pour this over the spinach and allow to cool and then after this, squeeze all water from the spinach.

5. Then fry the potato and onion in heated oil in skillet for ten minutes till potato become tender. Then take the eggs and beat them together in a bowl and add the salt and pepper according to your own choice. Take spinach and mix it into potatoes.

6. Then right after this, pour in eggs and cook, mixing from time to time. Then after this, flash omelet below grill to set the top. Then move the omelet to a dish and then after this, turn it over back in pan.

Grilled Goat's Cheese on Bed of Lettuce

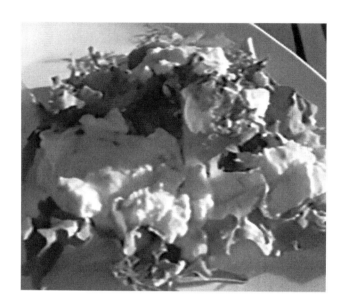

Ingredients

- 11 ounces goat cheese
- 1 tablespoon oil
- 4 cups Baby Spinach
- Vinaigrette
- 1/2 cup virgin olive oil
- 3 tablespoons sherry wine vinegar
- 1 tablespoon honey
- Salt and pepper

Directions

1. For vinaigrette, take the pepper, salt, honey and dissolve them in vinegar and then beat in virgin olive oil till emulsified.

2. Then chop the cheese into thick slices and grill them till become golden in color.

3. Take the baby greens and put them on dishes and then use the vinaigrette as dressing and then add the cheese over it.

Chicken and Peppers in Garlic Wine Sauce

Ingredients

- 2 lbs chicken breasts, boneless skinless
- 5 -6 tablespoons extra virgin olive oil
- 4 -5 garlic cloves, peeled and sliced
- 2 red bell peppers, roasted
- 12 -20 ounces dry white wine

Directions

1. First of all, take the chicken breast and salt them on both of the sides. Then take the olive oil and pour this into skillet and then put on moderate temperature setting. Then put the chicken breasts in the skillets and cook them on both of the sides. Take the garlic and add this to skillet and fry with chicken over low temperature setting.

2. Take the peppers and chop them into strips and put them in skillet. Take TWELVE ounces white wine and put this into skillet and cook over moderate temperature setting till ready and done.

3. Then after this, chop the chicken into slices and put them on a dish along with red pepper and garlic slices. Then take the wine sauce and pour this over the top.

Stuffed Bell Peppers

Ingredients

- 4 bell peppers
- 1/2 cup rice
- 1/2 lb hamburger
- 1 larger white onion
- 3/4 cup diced canned tomato
- 3/4 cup water
- 3 tablespoons Spanish basil
- 2 tablespoons Spanish oregano
- 2 tablespoons Spanish chili powder
- 2 tablespoons Spanish paprika

- 2 tablespoons Spanish black pepper
- 5 garlic cloves
- 3 tablespoons Spanish garlic powder
- 1/4 cup white cheese
- 1/4 cup orange cheese

Directions

1. Cook the rice and onions in skillet till become brown in color. Take water and add it to cover for nine minutes then sauté the hamburger with one tablespoon of each of the seasoning. Once hamburger is almost done, you can now add the rice as well as tomatoes.

2. Then after this, you can add the remaining items besides garlic powder. Then cook for five minutes then after this, gut the pepper out and then use the garlic powder for dusting. Take the rice mixture and layer it with the cheese when stuffing the bell peppers.

3. Then after this, enclose with top and put on cooking sheet. Then bake for approximately ¾ hour and then remove from oven and allow to cool properly well.

Mackerel (Or Tuna) and Red Pepper Stew

Ingredients

- 1 tablespoon olive oil
- 1 onion, chopped
- 1 garlic clove
- 1 teaspoon dried chili
- 1/4 pint white wine
- 400 g chopped tomatoes
- 1 lb potato, cubed
- 1 teaspoon paprika
- 1 juicy red pepper
- 2 mackerel fillets, cut into chunks or 2 tuna fillets, flaked or 2 pieces chunks chorizo sausage
- Chopped fresh coriander

Directions

1. First of all, cook the onions till become soft in heated oil then after this, take chili, garlic and add them and mix for sixty seconds and then right after this, pour in wine. Then pour in tomatoes. Then pour in potatoes then use the paprika as sprinkle and blend them well.

2. Take half tomato tin of water and add it and allow to simmer, covered, for approximately twenty five minutes or till potatoes are ready and done. Then after this, grill the peppers then put in plastic back till skin can be easily removed. Then after this, slice and put to the pan along with chorizo/fish.

3. Allow to simmer till ready and done. Then use the paprika and coriander as sprinkles.

Spanish Seafood Paella

Ingredients

- 6 cups reduced-sodium chicken broth
- 1/2 teaspoon saffron thread, crumbled
- 1/8 teaspoon ground pepper
- 1/4 teaspoon paprika
- 2 tablespoons olive oil
- 1 1/4 cups diced green peppers
- 1 cup sliced onion
- 3 garlic cloves, minced
- 1 1/2 cups Arborio rice or 1 1/2 cups short-grain rice
- 1/2 lb peeled deveined medium raw shrimp
- 1/2 lb bay scallop
- 2 cups diced plum tomatoes
- 1 (11 ounce) cans Mexican-style corn

Directions

1. Mix the 1ˢᵗ four items in saucepan. Heat to boiling and then lower the temperature and allow to simmer for ten minutes Then after this, fry the garlic, onion and green pepper in heated olive oil for five minutes, mixing continuously, till become slightly brown in color

2. Then take rice and add it and cook for sixty seconds, mixing continuously. Then blend in broth mixture and allow to simmer for 1/3 hour, mixing from time to time.

3. Then blend in shrimp and rest of items. Then allow to simmer for ten minutes or till liquid is assimilated and absorbed.

Paella-Style Shellfish Pasta

Ingredients

- 2 cups chicken broth
- 3/4 cup dry white wine
- 1/2 teaspoon saffron thread
- 3 tablespoons olive oil
- 6 ounces fideos or 6 ounces thin spaghetti, either pasta broken into 2-inch lengths
- 6 large shrimp, shelled
- 6 large sea scallops
- 6 clams, scrubbed
- 4 ounces frozen artichoke hearts, thawed
- 1 teaspoon chives

Directions

1. First of all, heat the wine and broth to boiling saucepan and blend in saffron. Then after this, fry the uncooked pasta in oil in sauté pan over medium high temperature setting, mixing from time to time till become golden in color, takes approximately. two minutes

2. Take the simmering broth mixture and pour this over the pasta and allow to simmer for five minutes take the shellfish, artichoke hearts and nestle them into pasta and bake in the centre of oven for approximately 1/3 hour.

3. Use the chives as sprinkle over the pasta.

Spanish Rice Casserole

Ingredients

- 1 lb ground beef
- 1 onion, finely chopped
- 1 -2 tablespoon fresh minced garlic
- 1 small green bell pepper, chopped
- 1 (14 1/2 ounce) cans Tomatoes (drained)
- 1 cup water
- 1/2-3/4 cup uncooked long-grain rice
- 1/2 cup chili sauce
- Salt and pepper
- 1 -2 teaspoon brown sugar
- 1 teaspoon cumin (or to taste)
- 2 -3 teaspoons Worcestershire sauce

- 1 1/2 cups shredded cheddar cheese (can use more)
- 3 tablespoons chopped fresh cilantro (optional and to taste)

Directions

1. First of all, cook the ground beef in sauté pan over moderately high temperature setting, then drain fat and then shift the beef to pot over moderately low temperature setting. Then blend in onion then blend in garlic green pepper and then blend in tomatoes. Then blend in water and then blend in rice.

2. Then blend in chili sauce. Then blend in salt and pepper. Then blend in brown sugar. Then blend in Worcestershire sauce. Then blend in cuminutes Allow to simmer for approximately. HALF hour, mixing from time to time then shift to prepared casserole dish and press the mixture.

3. Then after this, bake at three hundred fifty (35o) degrees Fahrenheit for ¼ hour or till cheese is melted. Use the cilantro as garnish.

Almond-Crusted Catalan Chicken

Ingredients

- 1 cut-up broiler-fryer chicken, skinned
- 1/4 cup mayonnaise
- 3 garlic cloves, finely minced
- 2 tablespoons fresh orange juice
- 2 teaspoons freshly grated orange rind
- 2 teaspoons honey
- 1/4 teaspoon cinnamon, divided

- 3/4 teaspoon salt, divided
- 1/2 teaspoon pepper, divided
- 1 cup fine dry plain breadcrumbs
- 1/2 cup sliced almonds
- 3 tablespoons olive oil

Directions

1. Prepare the marinade, by blending the mayonnaise, 1/4 teaspoon of the salt and 1/4 teaspoon of the pepper, garlic, orange juice, orange peel, honey, 1/8 teaspoon of the cinnamon in a bowl.

2. Take the chicken and add it and turn well for proper coating then keep in refrigerator, covered, for sixty minutes, spoon the marinade over the chicken from time to time. Take the rest of cinnamon, salt, pepper, breadcrumbs, almonds and olive oil & blend them together in pie pan.

3. Then take out the chicken of marinade and roll in the bread crumb mixture. Then put the chicken in one layer in the baking pan that has been greased. Then bake for sixty minutes at three hundred fifty (350) degrees Fahrenheit or till become crunchy and brown in color.

Caldo Gallego

Ingredients

- 3/4 cup dried great northern beans
- 8 cups water
- 1/2 lb chorizo sausage, sliced
- 1/4 lb salt pork or 1/4 lb bacon, diced
- 2 turnips, peeled and sliced
- 1 medium red onion, sliced
- 1 garlic clove, minced
- 1 teaspoon salt
- 1/4 teaspoon pepper
- 1 (10 ounce) packages frozen turnip greens or 1 (10 ounce) packages frozen chopped spinach
- 1 cup cabbage, chopped

Directions

1. Take beans, four cups water and mix them together in Dutch oven. And heat to boiling and then lower the temperature and allow to simmer for 120 seconds and then take away from heat and allow to rest, covered, for sixty minutes then drain and rinse the beans.

2. Take the rest of four cups of water, rinsed beans and mix them together in the same Dutch oven and heat to boiling, then lower the temperature and allow to simmer, covered, for approximately ¾ hour. Then after this, cook the salt pork and sausage, till brown in color. Then drain.

3. Take the salt, pepper, garlic, sausage, salt pork, turnips, red onion, and add them to beans and bring back to boiling, then lower the temperature and allow to simmer, covered, for 1/3 hour. Take the spinach, cabbage and add them and bring back to boiling and then lower the temperature and allow to simmer for extra ten minutes or till become soft.

Paella with Chicken, Zucchini and Rosemary

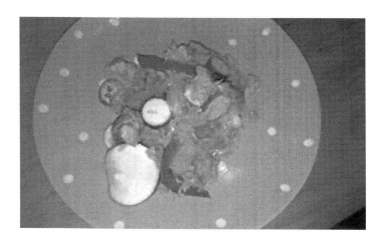

Ingredients

- 3/4 cup olive oil
- 2 1/2 lbs chicken, boneless skinless breasts, cut into pieces
- 1 large onion, chopped
- 5 garlic cloves, minced
- 1 large green pepper, chopped
- 3 ounces dry sherry
- 1 1/2 cups rice, uncooked
- 3 cups chicken broth
- 1/4 teaspoon saffron
- 1/4 teaspoon turmeric
- 3 tablespoons fresh rosemary, chopped
- 3 large zucchini, cut into 1 inch strips
- Salt and pepper, to taste

Directions

1. Cook the chicken in one fourth cup of olive oil in skillet till ready and done and brown in color on each of the side. And put aside and then clean the skillet and cook the onion in rest of olive oil over moderate temperature setting for four to six minutes take the green pepper, garlic and add them and cook for 3 minutes

2. Take sherry and add it and cook for next sixty seconds then right after this, pour in rice and fry for four to six minutes then blend in broth. Then blend in saffron. Then blend in turmeric. Then blend in browned chicken and then blend in 1.5 tbsp of rosemary and cook for ¼ hour.

3. Then use the rest of rosemary as sprinkle and mix. Take the zucchini and organize over rice and cook, covered for next ten minutes or till chicken and rice become soft and broth is assimilated and let it cool for a while.

Vegetable Brown Rice

Ingredients

- 2 cups water
- 1 cup uncooked brown rice
- 1/2 teaspoon dried basil
- 2 medium carrots, scrubbed and cut into thin 1 inch strips
- 1 cup chopped onion
- 9 green onions, cut into 1 inch strips
- 1/2 cup raisins
- 2 tablespoons olive oil
- 1 (10 ounce) packages frozen peas, thawed
- 1 teaspoon salt
- 1 cup pecan halves, toasted

Directions

1. Heat the water to boiling in moderate saucepan. Blend in rice. Then blend in basil. Then lower the temperature and allow to simmer, covered, for ¾ hour or till rice become soft.

2. Then sauté and mix carrots, green onions and onion in heated oil for five minutes or till veggies become brown in color. Take the salt, peas and add them and cook for sixty seconds or till veggies become soft

3. Blend in pecans. Then blend in raisins. Then blend in rice and heated through.

Spanish Chicken with Rice and Olives

Ingredients

- 9 chicken pieces (can use less)
- Seasoning salt (or use white salt)
- Pepper
- 4 -6 tablespoons olive oil
- 1 large onion, chopped
- 2 tablespoons fresh minced garlic
- 1 large red bell pepper, seeded and chopped
- 2 teaspoons paprika (can use more)
- 2 teaspoons dried red pepper flakes (optional or to taste)
- 2 cups uncooked converted white rice
- 1 1/4 cups dry white wine
- 1 (14 ounce) cans diced tomatoes with juice

- 3 1/2 cups chicken broth
- 3/4 teaspoon saffron thread
- 1 bay leaf
- 1 1/2 cups frozen peas
- 1/2 cup pimento-stuffed green olives, sliced (or to taste)

Directions

1. Add the salt as well as pepper to the chicken pieces. Then after this, cook the chicken in heated oil in sauté pan over moderately high temperature setting on both of the sides and then move to a dish. Take the dried chili flakes, red bell pepper, and garlic and add them and fry them for five minutes

2. Then take the rice, paprika, garlic and add them and fry for three minutes, mixing. Take wine and add it and heat to boiling, then allow to simmer for three minutes Then take the bay leaf, tomatoes with juice, saffron, chicken broth and add them and allow to simmer for six minutes then bring the chicken back from bowl to sauté pan along with any of the juices and then after this, nestle into rice.

3. Then right after this, cook, covered, over low temperature setting till chicken is done. Then after this, take olives, peas and add them and add salt and pepper according to your own choice. And allow to sit the sauté pan, covered, for ten minutes

Beef Cubes in Sherry

Ingredients

- 2 tablespoons olive oil
- 2 lbs lean stewing beef, cubed
- 1 (1 1/4 ounce) packages onion soup mix
- 1 cup sherry wine
- 1 teaspoon garlic salt
- 1/4 lb sliced mushrooms

Directions

1. Cook the beef cubes in heated oil on each of the side. Take the mushrooms, garlic salt, sherry, soup mix and add them and blend well.

2. Then after this, cover pot and allow to simmer the mixture for a minimum of sixty minutes or till meat become soft.

Vueltas de Carne

Ingredients

- 3 lbs top round steaks, very thinly sliced
- 6 cloves garlic, quartered and sliced thinly
- 1/2 cup chopped parsley
- 4 tablespoons olive oil
- 1 teaspoon red wine vinegar (or less) or 1 1/2 tablespoons white wine
- Salt and pepper

Directions

1. Take the steaks and pound them till they become thin. Then add the salt and pepper on each side of the steaks. Take the rest of items and mix them together and brush over the steaks. Then let it marinate for a minimum of thirty minutes

2. Sauté these steaks in olive oil over high temperature setting per side till lose its pink. Then discard any of the burned garlic. Then shift the steaks to a pot and cover.

Lamb Chops (Or Cutlets) W/Caramelized Garlic

Ingredients

- 8 (4 ounce) lamb chops (or cutlets, each weighing approximately 4 oz.)
- Salt (to taste)
- Pepper (to taste)
- 1/4 cup olive oil
- 24 garlic cloves
- 2 ounces red wine

Directions

1. First of all, sauté the garlic cloves in heated olive oil till golden brown in color and take out of sauté pan. Then after this, in the same sauté pan, sauté the rinsed, cleaned and seasoned lamb chops each side till slightly pink in color in the middle.

2. Take out the chops to a dish and then after this, pour off any additional oil in the sauté pan. Then use the two ounces red wine for deglazing the pan drippings and bring the garlic cloves back to the pan for short period of time.

3. Then after this, take the pan juices, garlic cloves and pour them over lamb chops

Delicious Spanish Burger

Ingredients

- 1 1/2 lbs ground chuck
- Salt & freshly ground black pepper
- 4 manchego cheese, cubes cut 1x1/2x1/2-inch each
- 4 slices serrano ham
- 1 tablespoon olive oil

Directions

1. First of all, layer the ground chuck in one layer and add the salt and pepper and then distribute the chuck into four parts. Then after this, take the each piece of manchego and wrap it in square piece of ham.

2. Sauté the each ham and cheese bundle in heated oil over moderate temperature setting, turning, till ham is crunchy and cheese melts then let cool. Take the meat and fold it around each bundle for making hamburgers.

3. Then after this, grill the burgers on high temperature setting for five minutes each side or till done.

If you enjoy the recipes in this little recipe book, please take the time to share your thoughts and post a review on Amazon. It'd be greatly appreciated!

Thank you and good luck!

Victoria Love
www.AfflatusPublishing.com
www.epicdetox.com
www.secretstoweightlossrevealed.com

Check Out My Other Books

Below you'll find some of my other popular books that are popular on Amazon and Kindle as well. You can visit my author page on Amazon to see other work done by me.

Paleo: The Caveman's Paleo For Beginners: Amazing! The Ultimate Paleo Diet for Beginner's Blueprint for Incredible Caveman's Revenge Paleo Cookbook: 41 Red Hot Melt The Pounds Fast Weight Loss Recipes Uncovered With Your Top Paleo Diet Questions Answered In Never Before Seen Detail

10 Day Green Smoothie Cleansing: The Ultimate Lose 10 Pounds in 10 Days Green Smoothie Detox Blueprint

10 Day Detox Diet: Innovative Diet Plan Transforms Your Life, Instantly Giving You Explosive Energy and Vitality Guaranteed

Vegetarian Slow Cooker Recipes Revealed: Fast Recipes For Slow Delicious Success

Cooking Light in 3 Steps; Cooking Light Has Never Been So Easy; Super-Fast and Light Done Right Cooking Revealed, Simple 3 Step Recipes, Fast Cooking Done Right

Famous Recipes Cookbook; Rediscover 70 All-Time Super Star Classic Recipes

Cookbooks Of The Week: Oy Mate! Australian Cooking From Down Under: 70 Amazingly Delicious Australian Cooking Recipes From the Outback and Beyond

Cookbooks Of The Week: No Wok Takeout; 80 Chinese Cooking Uncovered; 80 Secret, Delicious Ready-In-A-Snap Chinese Cooking Recipes Revealed

Cookbooks Of The Week: Japanese Cooking; 60 Super Easy, Amazingly Delicious Japanese Recipes Made Hot and Fast

You can simply search for these titles on the Amazon website to find them.

Your *Secret FREE Bonus!*

As a preferred client of Afflatus Publishing we strive to provide more value, all the time. As you are now a special part of our family we want to let you in on a little a little secret…

A special thanks goes out to you. So subscribe to our free e-book giveaway. Each week we will spotlight an amazing new title. *Yours absolutely free.*

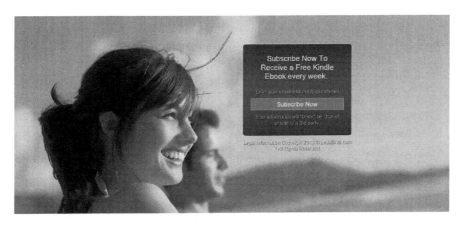

Subscribe For Free Now
https://afflatus.leadpages.net/free-ebook/

Made in the USA
Middletown, DE
20 March 2016